ADMIT IT ... LIFE WOULD BE BORING WITHOUT ME

SASSY & FUNNY QUOTES
ADULT COLORING BOOK

Enjoying this book?

Please leave a review because we would love to know your thoughts, feedback, and opinions to create better paper products for you!

Thank you so much for your support.

Life is short. Make every hair flip count.

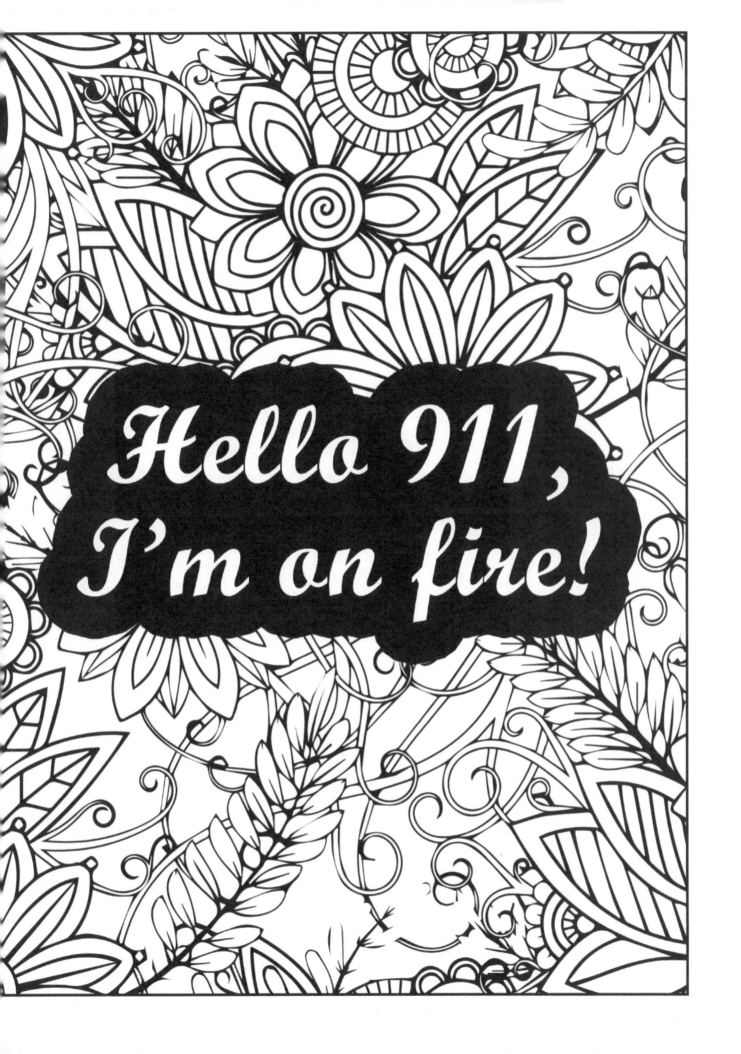

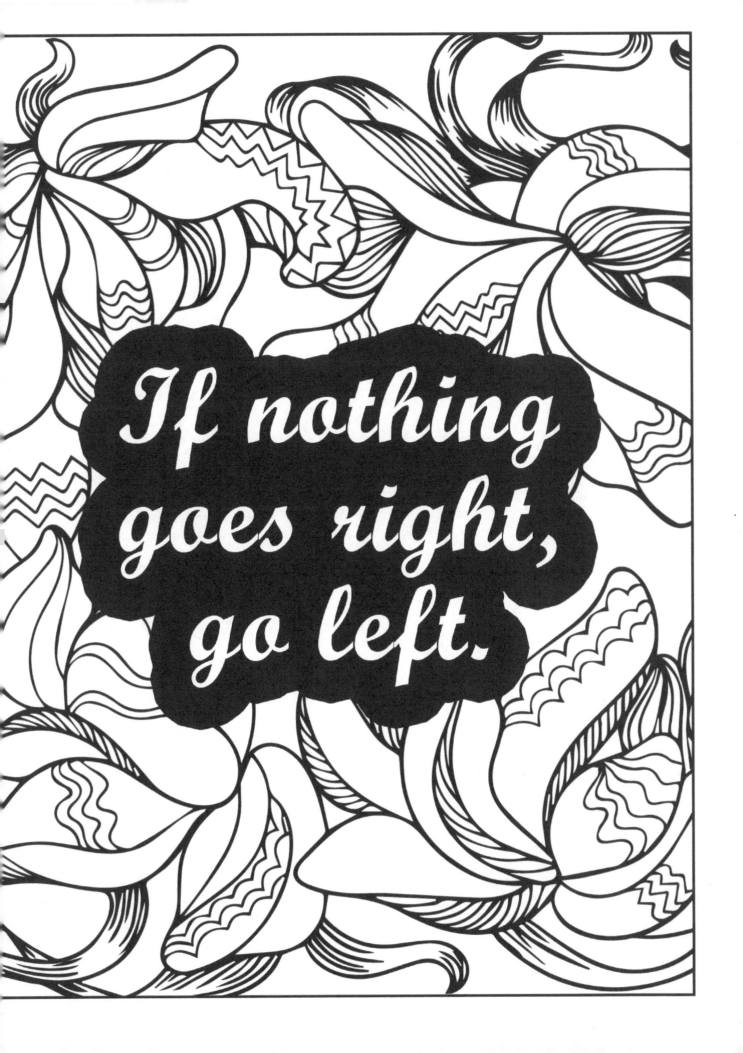

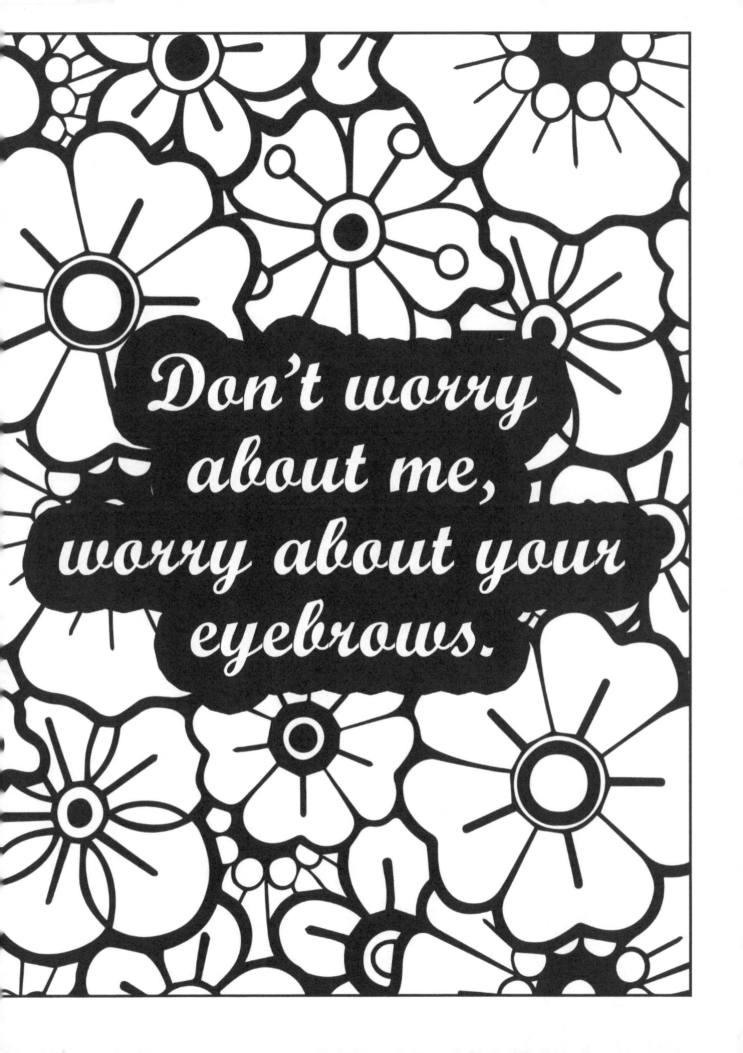

I like my coffee how I like myself: Dark, bitter, and too hot for you.

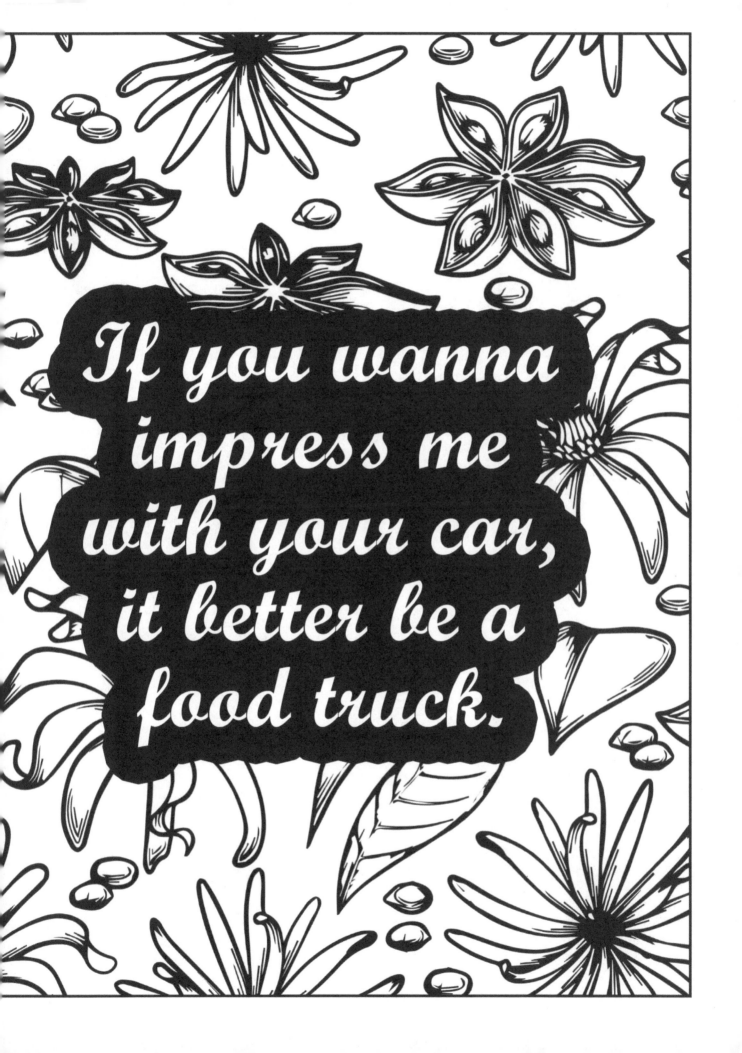

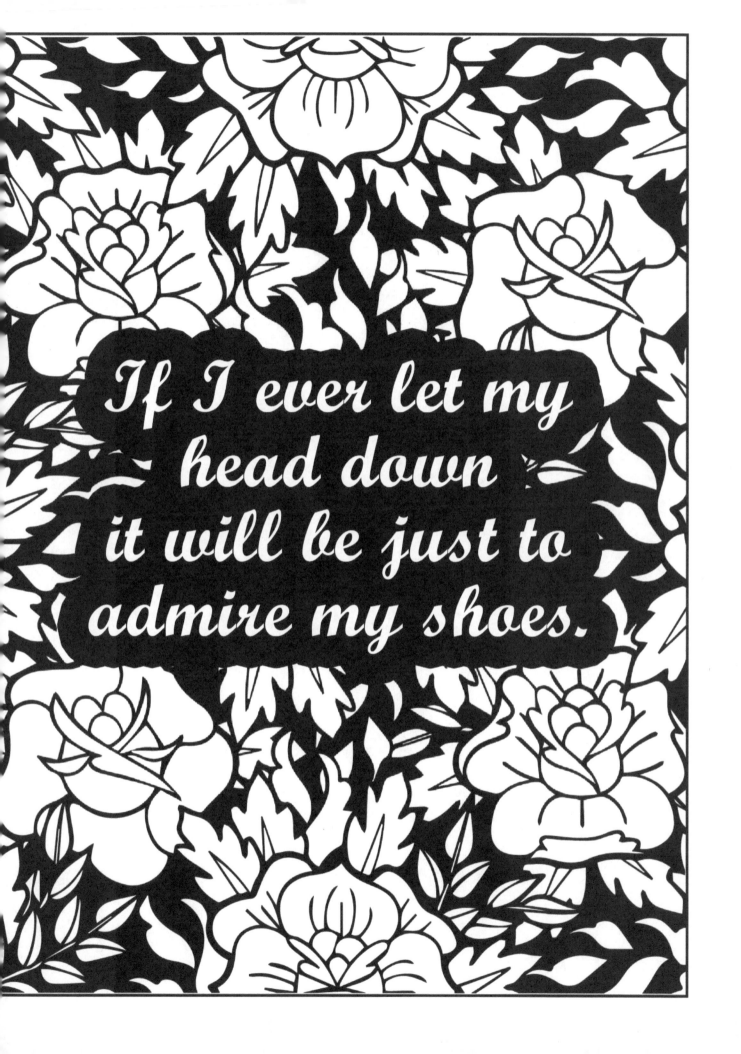

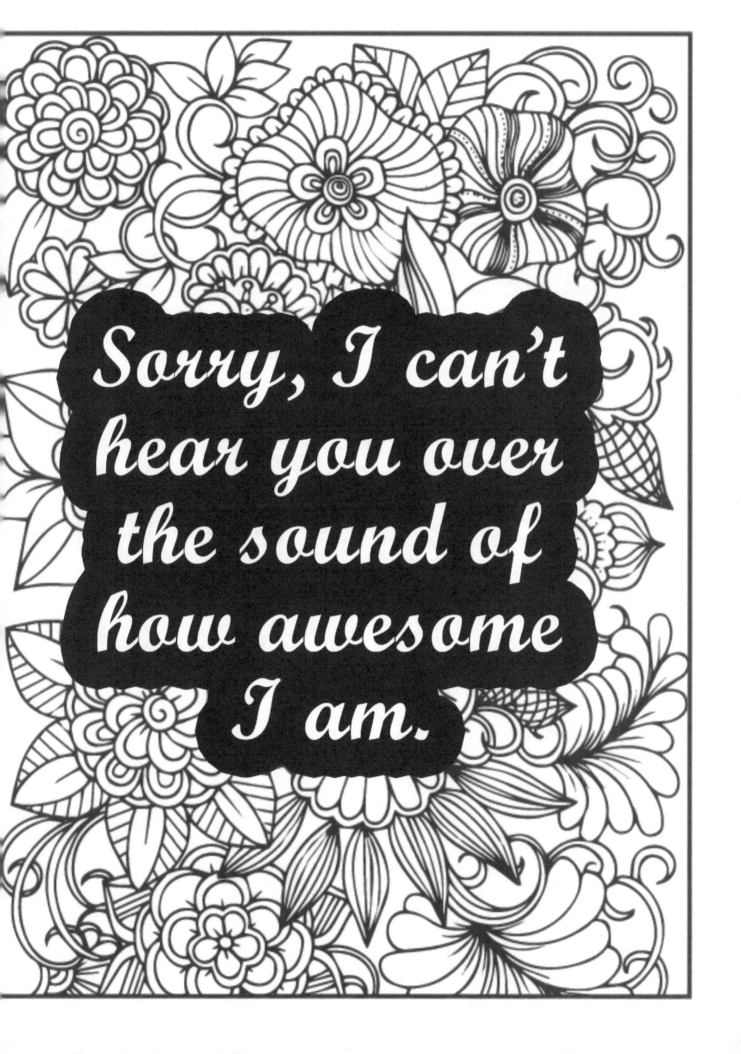

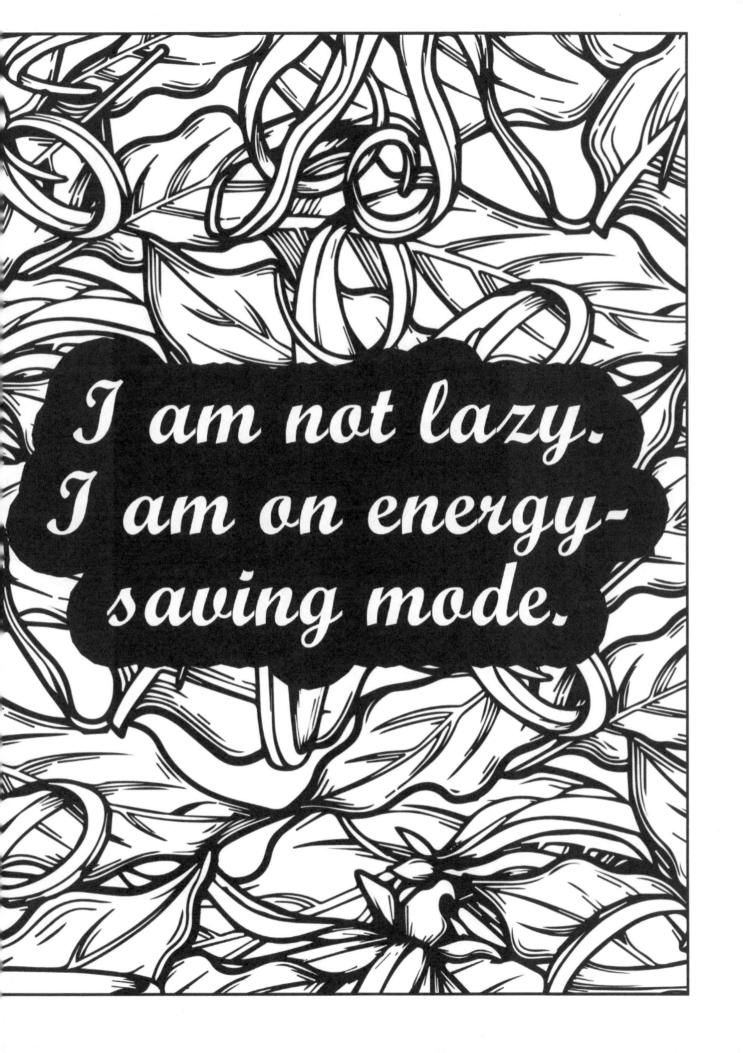

Sunshine mixed with a little hurricane.

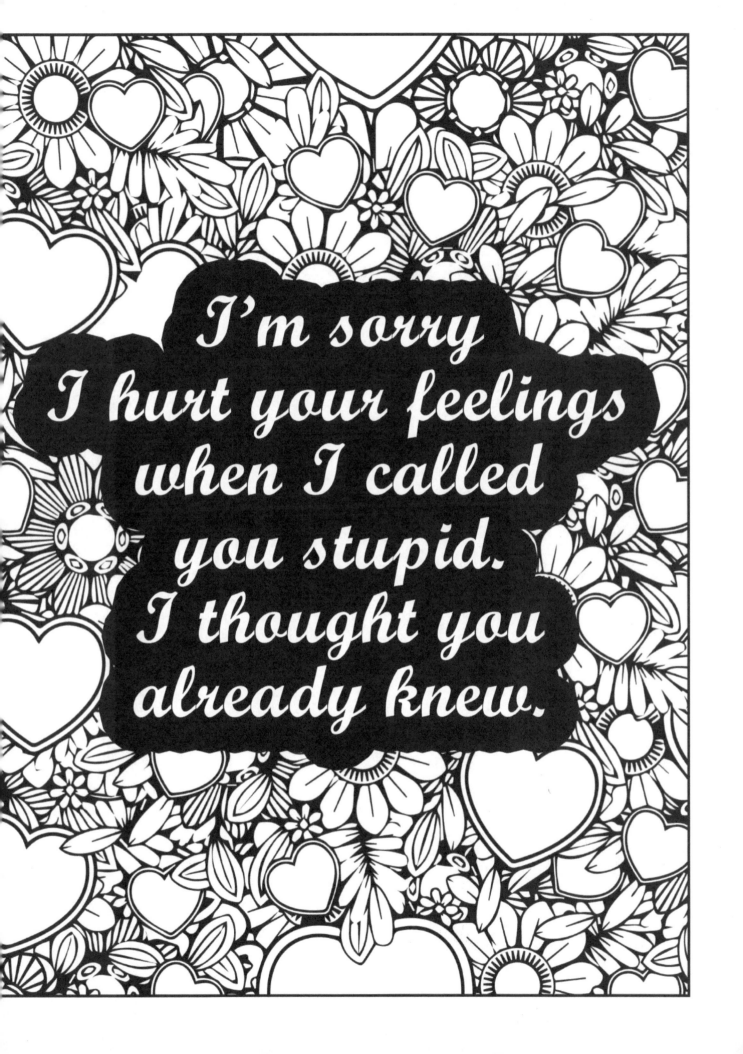

Some people just need a high five. In the face. With a chair.

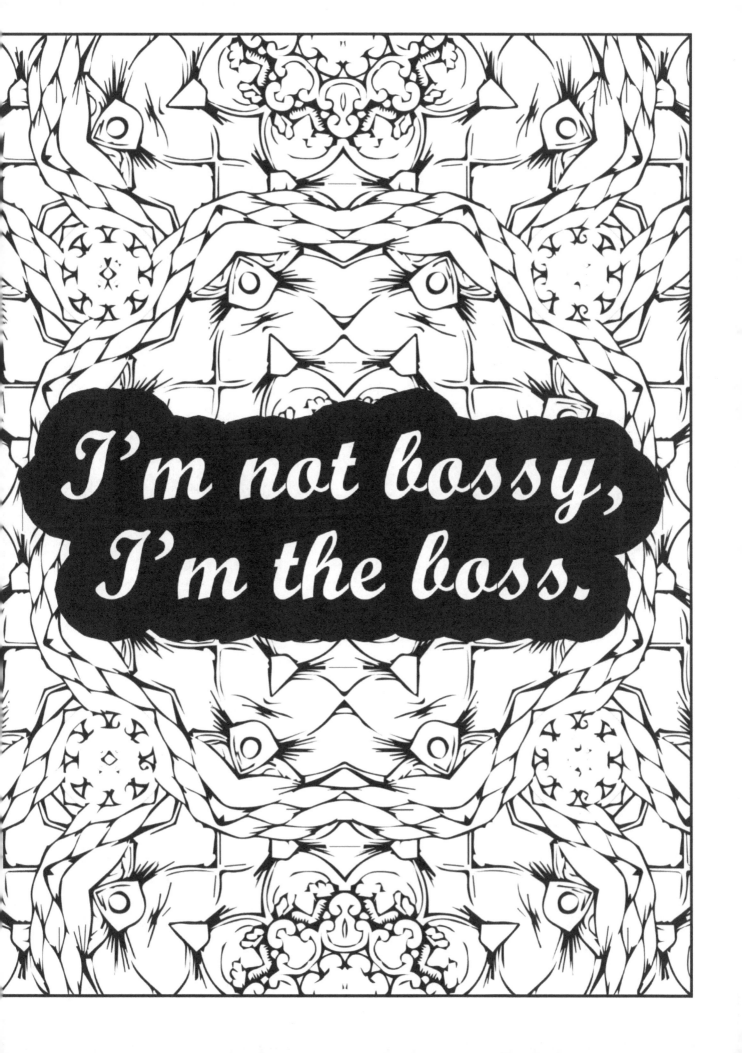

I'm not bossy, I'm the boss.

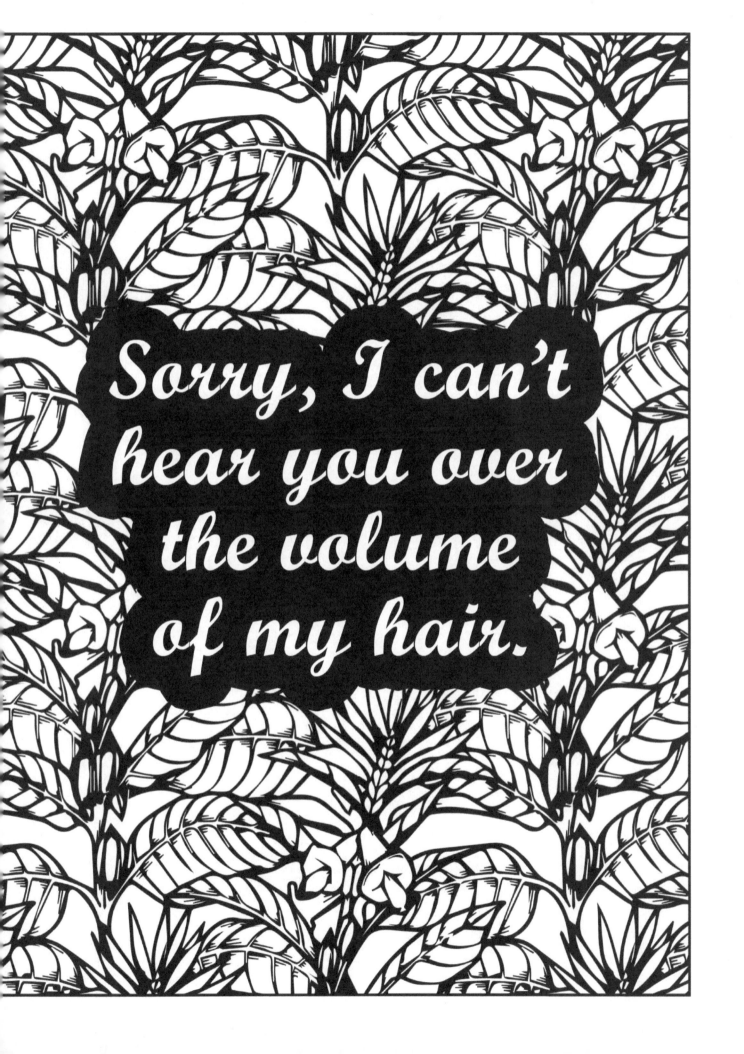

Made in United States
Troutdale, OR
12/20/2024

27045010R00031